A very scandi christmas
COLORING BOOK

@JenRacineColoringBooks

Jen Racine Coloring

Jen Racine.com

velkommen

and thank you for choosing a Jen Racine coloring book! In this book you will find 28 pages of Scandinavian-inspired Christmas artwork. These drawings are similar in style to my Scandi Nature, Time to Hygge and Modern Cottage Coloring books but with their own unique look and feel. I truly hope you find enjoyment and relaxation in these pages. Coloring either solo or with loved ones is a wonderful way to get into the spirit of the season.
Happy Coloring, friends!
- Jen

Use this tear out page in the back of the book to put behind your pages. This prevents indentation or transfer of ink to the pages below. The paper in this book is best suited for colored pencils or very light pens.

Find individual pages for sale in my Etsy shop:
etsy.com/shop/
JenRacineColoring

Copyright © 2023 by Eclectic Esquire Media LLC
ISBN: 978-1-958048-52-8

No part of this publication may be reproduced, distributed or transmitted in any form or by any means, without the prior written permission of the publisher, except in the case of brief quotations embodied in critical reviews and certain other noncommercial uses permitted by copyright law.

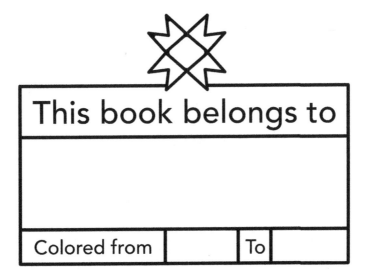

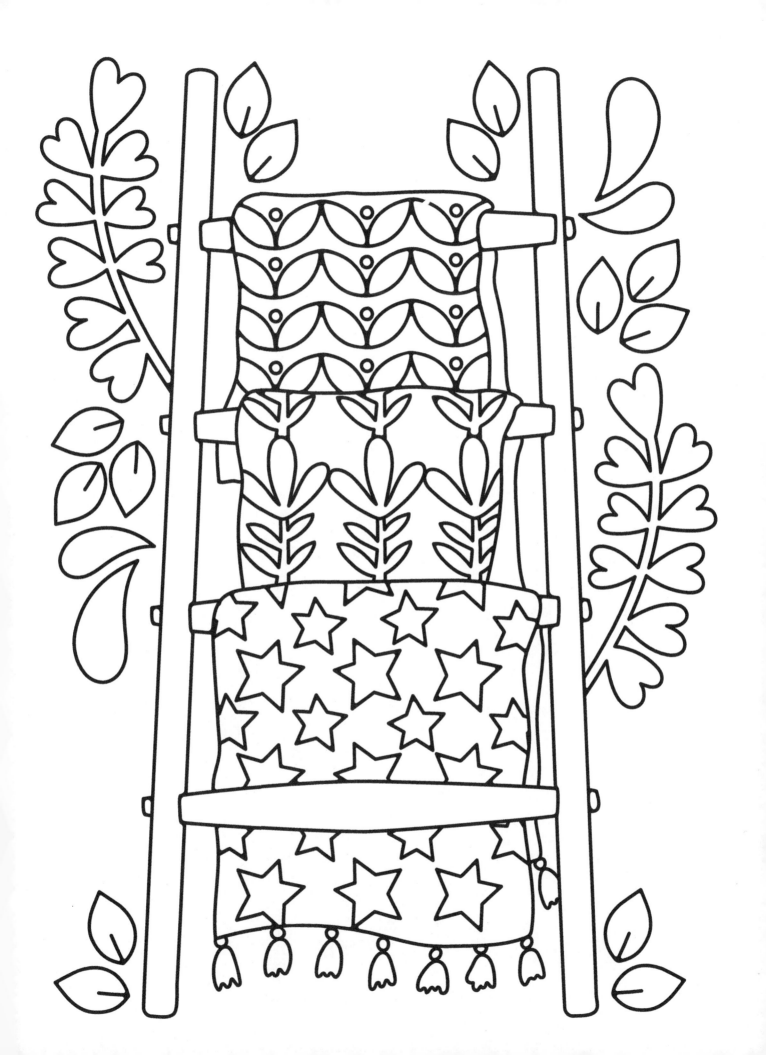

Made in the USA
Las Vegas, NV
08 December 2024